THE BOOK OF KELLS

A SELECTION OF PAGES REPRODUCED
WITH A DESCRIPTION AND NOTES BY
G. O. SIMMS

DUBLIN:
The Dolmen Press
& the Library of Trinity College

Distributed outside Ireland
by Oxford University Press

First impression 1961
Second impression 1963

tHE BOOK OF KELLS contains the four Gospels of the New Testament, St. Matthew, St. Mark, St. Luke, and St. John, written in Latin. In addition, there are Prefaces to the Gospels, Summaries (*breves causae*), Tables of reference numbers (*Eusebian Canons*)(see Plate 2), and part of a Glossary, giving the interpretation of Hebrew proper names.

The leaves or folios of the Book, numbering 340 in all, are made of thick-glazed vellum or parchment. The measurements of the pages are 13 inches by 9½ inches; before the pages were cut, the measurements were probably 15 inches by 11 inches. The Book is in an incomplete state; there are missing leaves both at the beginning and at the end.

The handwriting is bold, well-rounded and print-like (Plates 14, 16, 17, 18, 19). This expert Irish majuscule script is more formal than the cursive writing of the ordinary manuscripts of the same period. The Book of Kells is a manuscript de luxe, written and richly adorned for use in the conduct of public worship. The ink is brownish-black, but in the early pages, and at the end of St. Matthew's Gospel, red, bluish-black and purple inks were used

iii

alternately. There are usually seventeen lines on each page (sometimes eighteen, occasionally sixteen). Many of the letters are strongly reminiscent of modern Irish script; some are curiously distorted and elongated in order to fill out a line or to make a distinctive tailpiece.

THE ILLUMINATION

There is colour-illumination on all but two of the surviving pages (29v and 300v) of the book; thirty-one of these pages are fully illustrated. More generally, the decoration is confined to initial letters of paragraphs or sentences (Plate 18), to notable passages in the Gospels, e.g. the Genealogy of St. Luke (Plate 10), the Beatitudes in St. Matthew, and the famous Judgment passage in St. Matthew xxv, and also to the curved brackets of grotesque shape formed from animals and human figures, which indicate when words and syllables, not fitting into a line, have been placed above or below. These brackets were known familiarly among Irish scribes as 'the turn under the path' or 'the head under the wing'.

The colours used include: bright red, reddish purple, emerald green (malachite),

iv

deep blue (lapis lazuli) and yellow. The designs may be classified thus: *geometric* (these include circular patterns and the so-called trumpet pattern. In the latter, spirals expand into the shape of a trumpet, as in 29r); *zoomorphic* (animal-shaped); *phyllomorphic* (leaf-like patterns) and *figure-representations*.

SEVERAL ARTISTS

It is highly probable that more than one artist is responsible for the illumination. Mlle. Françoise Henry in her *Irish Art* suggests four possible artists. She assigns to one whom she calls 'the Goldsmith' the following:—

The Eight-Circle Cross (33r) (Plate 9), a master-piece of elaborate and delicate tracery, in which the colour and gloss of the parchment are used to great advantage by the artist. Here are drawn spirals, whorls, discs and dots, in addition to trumpet- and key-patterns, in designs which are never repeated. There is a theory that the four elements are symbolized in this style of ornamentation. Interlacings represent water, snakes earth, birds air, and the key-pattern fire.

v

The Chi Rho page (34r) (Plates 12, 13). The Greek Letters XPI form an abbreviation of Christi (St. Matthew 1, 18, 'the birth of Christ'). Abbreviations of sacred names appear throughout the book; only rarely are other words abbreviated. The dignity and sacredness of the names were emphasised in this way, e.g. IHS for Jesus, SPS SCS for Spiritus Sanctus (Holy Spirit), DS for Deus (God) and DNS for Dominus (Lord). The detail of the Chi Rho page repays careful study. In the left-hand bottom corner is the well-known cat and mouse scene, in which the cats are watching two mice nibbling sacred bread from the sanctuary, recalling perhaps an incident in the life of the monastery.

The Opening Pages of St. Matthew, St. Mark, and St. John.

Liber generationis. These are the first two words of St. Matthew's Gospel and are illuminated with great intricacy and gracefulness on 29r ('The book of the generation'). It is almost certain that the figure of an evangelist, supposedly St. Matthew, on the left of the page was not part of the original design.

The words *Initium Euangelii* IHU XPI ('The beginning of the Gospel of Jesus

vi

Christ') form the opening of St. Mark's Gospel and are the subject of a full-page illumination (130r) (Plate 3).

In *principio erat uerbum uerum* ('In the beginning was the true *(sic)* Word . . .', St. John 1, 1) is illuminated in similar style (292r).

PORTRAITS

Mlle. Henry suggests that a second artist whom she calls the 'Portraitist' is responsible for the three full-page figures of the Evangelists:

St. Matthew (28v).

St. John (291v), his head surrounded by a large nimbus, and a quill in his hand (Plate 8).

Portrait of Christ (32v)(Plate 1). The head is surmounted by a Cross. Two peacocks, one on each side of the head, stand on vines which issue from chalice-shaped vases. The style of hair and the swarthy features are characteristics of Celtic work.

Also assigned to the 'Portraitist' are the pages on which are portrayed in varying patterns the four traditional symbols of the Gospel-writers, (27v, 129v, 290v). (For the first of these, see Plate 11). The figure of a Man or an Angel represents St. Matthew and his treatment of Christ's human nature; the Lion for St. Mark, who writes of Christ's royal dignity; the Ox for St. Luke, who emphasises our Lord's sacrificial priesthood, and the Eagle for St. John, who 'soars to heaven.'

To the same artist is ascribed the 'Quoniam' page, the title page of St. Luke's Gospel (188r).

SCENES FROM THE GOSPEL

Yet another artist is said to be the 'Illustrator'. He depicts the well-known scenes in our Lord's life as follows:—

The Virgin and Child, displaying figures conventional and stiff, with a certain crudity of drawing (7v). (Plate 4).

The Temptation, showing our Lord with a rolled book in his hand, surmounting the Temple roof, in the presence of the Devil (202v). (Plate 7).

The Arrest. The figures of our Lord and the two who take him captive have a terrifying intensity and are somewhat grotesque. But the coiling patterns of the trefoil which indicated the divine presence and the snarling of the 'many dogs' who come about him strike most movingly the note of tragedy in the scene (114 r). (Plate 6).

The *Tunc crucifixerant* page (St. Matthew XXVII, 38) (124r) contains the words designed in the form of a St. Andrew Cross, *tunc crucifixerant XPI cum eo duos latrones* ('then they had crucified two thieves with him, Christ'). The word XPI is redundant and may have been put in to explain the word 'him'. There is no representation of the Crucifixion in the Book of Kells, but the page opposite this one is blank and may indicate that a crucifixion scene was intended (123v). (See Plate 15, which shows a little group of onlookers in the left-hand margin of the *Tunc crucifixerant* page gazing across at the blank page—intended perhaps by the artist to be watching the Crucifixion).

Yet a fourth style can be seen in the familiar pictures from everyday life which are dotted all over the manuscript and give the Book of Kells a special charm and fascination. An extensive list of animals, wild and domestic, birds, fishes as well as human figures, could be compiled. Plate 12 itself includes cats, mice, an otter, a fish, and a moth. A fish is also visible in Plate 14. Initial letters are ingeniously formed from animals wrestling, contorted human figures, fishes and lizard-like creatures. (Plates 14, 16, 17, 19, 20).   ix

Mention must also be made of the variety and beauty of the opening pages of the Book which contain reference figures and lists of parallel passages in the Gospels known as the Eusebian Canons. These are set out in the framework of Byzantine architecture with pillars, capitals, bases and tympana finely decorated. The oft-recurring theme of the symbols of the Four Evangelists is presented with ingenuity and beauty (Plate 2).

Much has been written about the different influences to be traced in the artistry of the Book. The haphazard nature of the decoration, the spontaneity and even the turbulence of writhing serpents and wrestling animals, the humorous incongruities, are all characteristic of Celtic work. Yet at the same time the precision and the accuracy of detailed design, when examined under a magnifying glass, are astounding. Oriental, especially Egyptian, influence may be seen in the features of the portrait subjects, in the colouring and treatment of the hair. Mlle. Henry suggests that the profuseness of the animal decoration is due to contact with painters in Gaul.

THE DATE

It is difficult to determine the date of the Book. It is generally supposed to belong to the eighth or early ninth century A.D. Some have concluded that it is as early as the seventh century. The most important evidence is furnished by the style of handwriting. The text itself (Codex Q) is that of the Vulgate intermingled with readings from the Old Latin; as was not uncommon in Irish manuscripts, explanations of words were placed in the text and appear as 'conflate readings' (e.g. St. Matthew VIII, 20 and IX, 32). Some supporting evidence of date is provided from the illustrations, e.g. a miniature of a warrior (200r) shows the small rounded shield in use before the coming of the Norsemen (see Plate 10).

There is a tradition that the workmanship was begun in Iona and finished in the Abbey at Kells in Co. Meath, some forty miles north-west of Dublin, by members of the Columban community who found refuge there after the Norse invasion of Iona. It is known that the Abbey at Kells was rebuilt in 804 A.D. after a fire, and that between 806 and 813 A.D. Cellach, the Abbot of Iona, took refuge in Kells.

The discoloration and damaged condition

of the Book may be accounted for by the incident recorded in the Annals of Ulster under the date 1006 A.D. as follows:

'The Great Gospel of Colum Cille was stolen at night from the western Erdomh (sacristy) of the great Church of Cean-nanus. This was the principal relic of the western world on account of its singular cover; and it was found after twenty nights and two months, its gold having been stolen off it, and a sod over it'. (J. O'Donovan's trans.)

Preserved in the blank pages and margins of the Book are seven charters written in the Irish language concerning property granted to the Abbey of Kells. Some of these date from the 11th century and prove that the ancient Irish committed their covenants to writing before the Anglo-Norman in-vasion. Such documents were often kept for safety in this way in the sacred books of a monastery.

After the Columban foundation came to an end in the twelfth century, the Book was preserved in the parish church of Kells, and there is evidence that James Ussher, when bishop-elect of Meath, inspected the Book and counted its leaves on August 24, 1621 (334v). During the Cromwellian period it

xii

was moved for safety to Dublin, and it is extremely probable that it was presented to the Library of Trinity College by Henry Jones, Bishop of Meath (1661-1682), the donor of the Book of Durrow. A facsimile was made in 1950, in two volumes with a third, introductory, volume giving much additional information. In 1953 the Book of Kells was repaired and rebound in four volumes by Roger Powell.

BIBLIOGRAPHY

THE BOOK OF KELLS: Facsimile edition (48 pages in colour). Berne, Urs Graf-Verlag, 1950.

ZIMMERMAN, E.H.: Vorkarolingische Miniaturen. Berlin, 1916.

HENRY, Françoise: Irish Art. London, 1940.

SULLIVAN, E.: Book of Kells, 5th ed. London, 1952.

ABBOTT, T. K.: Celtic Ornaments in the Book of Kells. Dublin and London. 1895.

ROBINSON, Stanford F.H.: Celtic Illuminative Art in the Gospel Books of Durrow, Lindisfarne, and Kells. Dublin, 1908.

GWYNN, A.: Some notes on the history of the Book of Kells. (*Irish Historical Studies*, vol. IX, No. 34, 1954).

POWELL, Roger: The Book of Kells: The Book of Durrow. Comments on the Vellum, the Make-up and Other Aspects. (*Scriptorium*, X, 1956).

O'SULLIVAN, William: The Donor of the Book of Kells. (*Irish Historical Studies*, vol. XI, No. 41, 1958).

THE PLATES

1

2

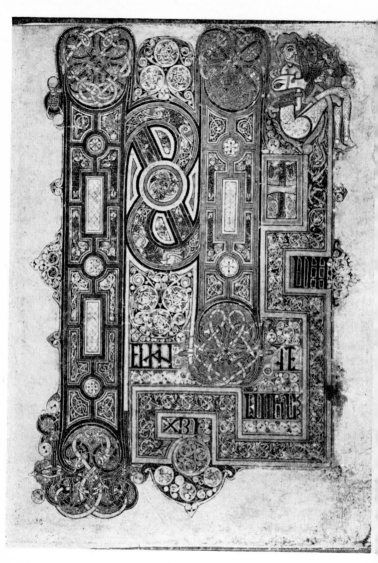

3

4

5

6

7

8

9

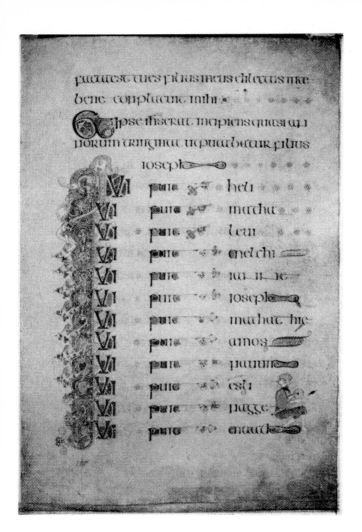

puditest tues filius meus dilectus me
bene complacuit mihi
Ipse ihseuit incipiens quasi an
norum triginta ut putabatur filius
ioseph

heli
mathat
leui
melchi
iannæ
ioseph
mathathie
amos
nauum
esli
nagge
enauth

11

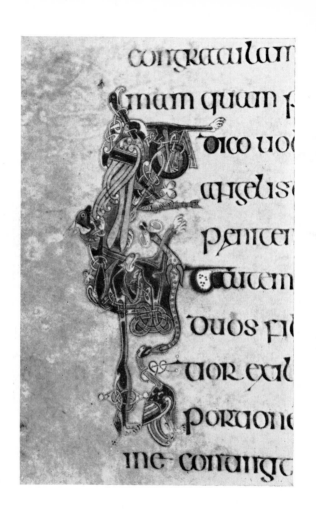

congratulam
nam quam p
oico uoo
angelis
pencer
aucm
ouos fi
uor exil
porаone
ne conungc

14

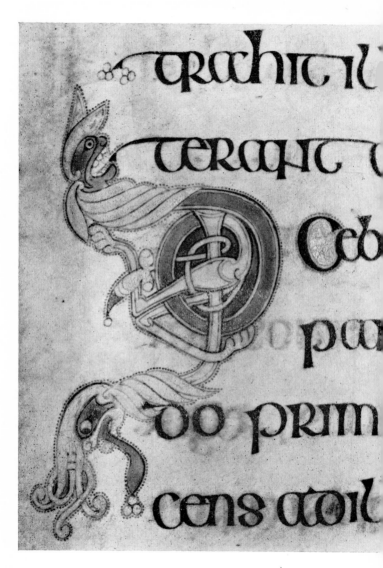

orahtil

teracht

Ceb

pa

oo prim

cens adil

16

les honpuifasq

emo serut

minis serui

cucrerum chi

cul ocerin cop

oiebant h

erant aua

cat illis uos

uos coran hom

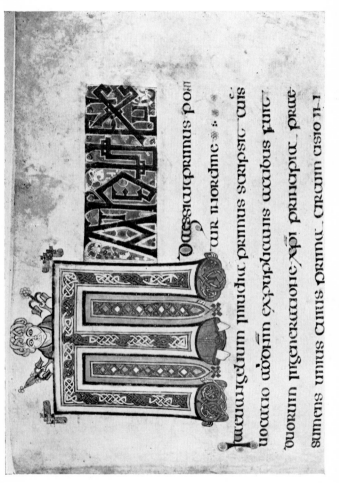

muta autem sunt u

eleca

cabentes

sibrum fecerū

eum ipsermone

20